WE BUILT THIS CITY

CHICAGO
History, People, Landmarks

THE WORLD'S FAIR, WRIGLEY FIELD, FRANK LLOYD WRIGHT

TAMRA B. ORR

Paperback ISBN 979-8-89094-046-9
Hardcover ISBN 979-8-89094-047- 6

Library of Congress Control Number: 2023943819

To learn more about the other great books from Fox Chapel Publishing, or to find a retailer near you, call toll-free 800-457-9112 or visit us at *www.FoxChapelPublishing.com*.

We are always looking for talented authors. To submit an idea, please send a brief inquiry to acquisitions@foxchapelpublishing.com.

Fox Chapel Publishing makes every effort to use environmentally friendly paper for printing.

Printed in China

ABOUT THE AUTHOR: Tamra B. Orr is a full-time author. She has written more than 500 educational books for readers of all ages. A graduate of Ball State University in Muncie, Indiana, Orr is a mother of four, an avid letter writer, and a travel enthusiast! She loves to hop in the car for long road trips, visiting the most interesting cities in America.

CHICAGO

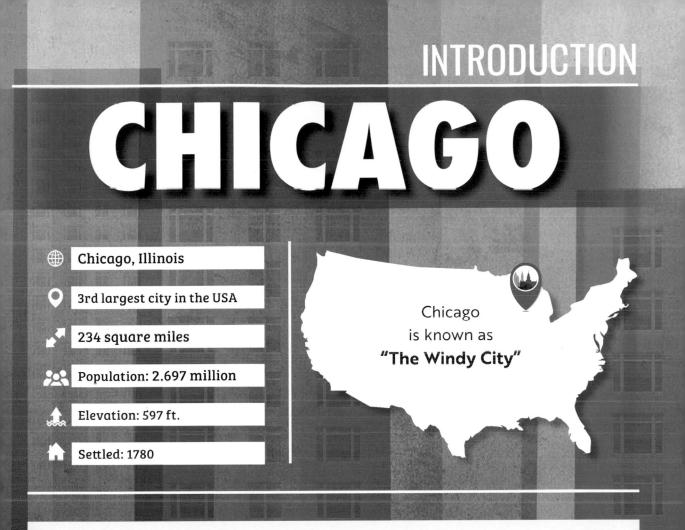

- 🌐 **Chicago, Illinois**
- 📍 3rd largest city in the USA
- ↗ 234 square miles
- 👥 Population: 2.697 million
- ⬆ Elevation: 597 ft.
- 🏠 Settled: 1780

Chicago
is known as
"The Windy City"

Renowned for its distinctive blend of history and modernity, Chicago stands as an iconic metropolis in the heart of America's Midwest. From its humble origins as a fur trading post to its rise as a bustling hub of industry and commerce, the city has been a microcosm of the changing face of America. Chicago is a thriving center for innovation and learning, home to world-class universities, a dynamic arts scene, and hundreds of unique cultural celebrations. With its soaring skyscrapers, vibrant neighborhoods, and a waterfront that rivals coastal cities, Chicago offers a unique blend of culture, architecture, and culinary delights. Explore this city's diverse communities, iconic landmarks, and the rich tapestry of its history. Welcome to Chicago!

CONTENTS

Souvenir Map OF THE WORLD'S COLUMBIAN EXPOSITION AT JACKSON PARK AND Midway Plaisance CHICAGO ILL. U.S.A. 1893

Top: Many visitors purchased colorful maps to preserve their memories of the fair. Some visitors even bought souvenir walking canes with maps that rolled out from cane shafts. The huge Ferris wheel (bottom) and the sparkling white liberal arts building (middle) were just two of the features of the amazing World's Fair in Chicago.

Welcome to the World's Fair!

Welcome to the 1893 World's Fair! Step into Chicago's White City. Notice how all of the white-painted buildings seem to glow in the sunshine? That was the architect's design. It is why we call this the White City.

Plan to spend the day, folks. There are more than 200 buildings to explore, plus exotic food to try. There is an early version of Cracker Jack, the new sweet-and-salty snack of caramel, popcorn, and peanuts. There is Wrigley's new Juicy Fruit gum. And don't miss what happens when the sun sets. The entire park lights up. That's right—electricity! You've never seen anything like this fair—and all for only 50 cents.

Hop on G.W. Ferris Jr.'s 264-foot-tall Ferris wheel. You will be able to see all of Jackson Park spread out below you—if you are brave enough to open your eyes. While you are on the Midway, you will come face to face with an Egyptian temple. Look closer and see that the Egyptian workers are not building pyramids. They are operating telephone boards and laying telegraph lines. The Western Electric Company blended the old with the new. Just wait until you see all of the electric bulbs lighting up the temple! Don't worry, folks. These newfangled lights are a little scary and loud, but they are safe.

The Manufactures and Liberal Arts Building is the largest covered building in the world! It is over 200 feet tall. It covers 30 acres. Inside you will find everything from priceless jewels to new inventions

Tesla's 500-horsepower generator was one of the most amazing inventions he brought to the fair.

like the electric elevator. It carries you straight up to the roof.

Stop by the Machinery Hall and see Thomas Edison's kinetoscope. Moving pictures! Can you just imagine it?

Other inventors have brought their gadgets too. Nikola Tesla has a whole display of engines and motors. Elisha Gray has a fascinating machine. It can turn your handwriting into electrical impulses. Then, it sends your penciled words or drawings to another pencil that copies it!

So folks, hand over your tickets, and get ready for the experience of a lifetime. You will never forget what you see in the White City!

The 1893 World's Fair in Chicago was also known as the Columbian Exposition. It honored the 400th anniversary of Christopher Columbus landing in North America. More than 27 million

Part of the park was modeled after Venice, Italy. People could ride boats from the Palace of Mechanic Arts (Machinery Hall) to other sections of the fair.

people came to Chicago to see it. That is an amazing 15,000 people every day!

Chicago was thrilled to host the fair. It had competed against other cities and won. Organizers wanted to

The World's Fair's Palace of Fine Arts is a familiar building in Chicago. It now attracts thousands of visitors each year as the Museum of Science and Industry.

prove that Chicago was a modern city. They hoped it would become known as the "Metropolis of the West."

To support all the fair's workers and visitors, Chicago built many hotels and restaurants. They constructed the "L," or elevated train, to transport the workers to and from the site. Having the World's Fair changed the entire layout of Chicago—and brought it the attention it wanted. The styles used in the fair's buildings were copied when the city was redesigned in 1909. Banks and museums were modeled after the ones at the fair—or just moved from the fairgrounds to the city. For example, the fair's Palace of Fine Arts is now Chicago's Museum of Science and Industry. The city's famed Art Institute was also originally built for the White City. As for the exhibits, many were donated or purchased for the future Field Museum.

Chicago has a rich history of blended cultures and forward thinkers. The World's Fair showcased those strengths and predicted how the city would continue to grow.

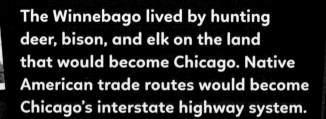

The Winnebago lived by hunting deer, bison, and elk on the land that would become Chicago. Native American trade routes would become Chicago's interstate highway system.

Settling the Area

Long before the World's Fair or Chicago or even Illinois existed, the land was home to a number of Native American groups. These included the Kickapoo, Miami, Ottawa, Potawatomi, Shawnee, and Winnebago. These groups hunted and fished, and some of them moved from place to place according to the season. Other groups settled down and built permanent villages. They made pottery and grew crops. As time passed, tribes grew larger. More villages were built. More time was spent on developing crops, including corn and vegetables.

From Missions to Forts

The first two non-Native Americans to explore the Chicago area were Frenchmen. Father Jacques Marquette and Louis Jolliet arrived in 1673. Marquette was a French missionary. Jolliet was a mapmaker and trader. They later settled in the area, inspiring other Europeans to follow.

The first non-Native American to settle in the future city of Chicago was a trader, Jean Baptiste Point du Sable. He was a free black man possibly from the country of Haiti. He and his Native American wife built a five-room home by the mouth of the Chicago River on Lake Michigan's shores. He ran a popular trading post there, attracting many people to the area.

In 1803, the U.S. Army built Fort Dearborn on the Chicago River's south bank. It was named after Henry Dearborn, who was President Thomas Jefferson's secretary of war. American soldiers and their

Fort Dearborn is such an important part of Chicago's history that it is represented both in the city's flag and in several plaques near the Michigan Avenue bridge.

families lived there. The fort was destroyed after a battle between the soldiers and the Potawatomi in 1812. It was rebuilt in 1816.

Becoming a City

As more military families moved to the area, trade increased. When Chicago's population hit 4,170 on March 4, 1837, it officially became a city. After that, changes came quickly.

The Illinois and Michigan Canal connected the Great Lakes and the Mississippi River. This made trade easier and faster. To keep up with the growth, Chicago also laid the tracks for its first railroad in 1848. The trains moved goods and grain much more quickly than horse-drawn carriages.

During the 19th century, many immigrants from around the world flocked to take advantage of the new opportunities in growing Chicago. People from places as varied as Germany, Poland, and China brought their traditions, popular dishes, and culture to Chicago, transforming the face of the city by settling in different neighborhoods, like Chinatown.

Germans arrive in Chicago. Immigrants from around the world greatly changed the city. They built churches, temples, and businesses like those in their homeland.

By 1870, the population had reached about 300,000. To fit in so many people, Chicago had to make some changes. First it had to solve a huge problem: mud. The entire city was built on a soggy marsh. A joke at the time described a person walking on the side of a road. He sees a gentleman whose head and shoulders are sticking out of the mud in the middle of the street. The person asks if he can help. The gentleman replies, "No thank you. I have a fine horse under me."

The mud was more than annoying. It bred disease. Cholera had already swept the city in 1854, killing thousands. The city tried hammering wooden planks over the mud. The mud seeped through and rotted the wood from underneath. Finally, in 1855, the city decided to install a sewer system.

Chicago was only a few feet above the level of nearby Lake Michigan. Underground sewers were not an option. There was not enough of a drop for them to be able to drain properly. Instead, the entire city would have to be raised 4 to 14 feet. For 20 years, the city worked to raise the buildings and give them stronger foundations. Some homes were moved elsewhere. A visitor told *The Chicago Tribune*, "Never a day passed ... that I did not meet one or more houses shifting their quarters. One day, I met nine."

Chicago was extremely proud of what it had done. It had every reason to be. However, hoisting the city used a great deal of wood. That was about to turn into a true disaster. In 1871, the city caught fire.

It took incredible effort and manpower to move a huge building such as the Briggs House Hotel.

Left: The map highlights the area burned by the fire. The red dot is where the fire started. It would be years before Mrs. O'Leary's cow was proven innocent of the massive fire in Chicago (top). People stormed across the Randolph Street Bridge, running for their lives (bottom).

Chapter Three

Disaster and Recovery

Just who started the Great Chicago fire? No one is quite sure.

Historians know when it started: October 8, 1871.

They know where it started: in the barn of Patrick and Catherine O'Leary.

They even know what started it: a knocked-over lantern. But who knocked it over?

For years people thought one of the O'Leary's cows did it. Others blamed it on a thief stealing milk. One man confessed he did it while running away from an illegal card game. In more recent years, a few scientists have suggested that a meteor shower started the hay burning. In 1997, the Chicago City Council issued a resolution announcing that poor Mrs. O'Leary and her cow were innocent all along. It was just a story that a reporter for the *Chicago Daily Tribune* had made up for the newspaper.

Regardless of how it started, the fire was one of the worst disasters in American history. It began on a windy October 8 and burned right through the heart of the city. Hot, dry weather and all the wooden buildings and sidewalks fueled the fire. One of the first buildings to burn down was the waterworks—the main water source for the fire department. To make matters worse, when the firetrucks headed out to address the fire, they went the wrong way!

The fire's destruction was overwhelming, but it inspired a number of changes in Chicago that would ultimately make it a safer city.

By the time the fire ended, more than 300 people had died. One-third of the entire city was homeless. About 17,500 buildings burned down. A day of hard rain helped put the fire out. By then, it had destroyed an area four miles long and almost one mile wide.

The Great Rebuilding Begins

Once the shock of the fire had passed, Chicago focused on recovering. All of the trash and wreckage was dumped into Lake Michigan. Six weeks later, 300 new buildings were already being built. The first "fireproof" building was built in 1873, and many of the other new buildings were also designed with fire prevention in mind. A new law had been passed to prevent future fires. Construction companies were told to use brick, stone, marble, and limestone instead of wood. Many home and small business owners could not afford these expensive materials. When a smaller fire hit Chicago in 1874, it destroyed more than 800 buildings. People then began using terra-cotta. This is an orange-brown sand-and-clay mixture that hardens to make tiles.

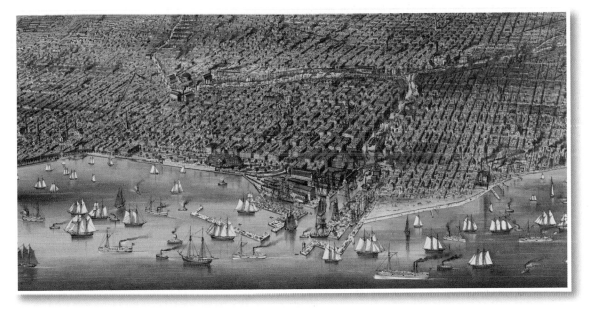

View of the city of Chicago showing the waterfront on Lake Michigan, and the newly rebuilt city following the 1871 Chicago Fire.

Terracotta is quite flameproof. It was used on so many buildings that Chicago was hailed as one of the world's most fireproof cities.

During the nineteenth century, Chicago grew quickly. Just two years after Chicago's first railroad was built, there were five. By 1856, there were ten. By the end of the century, dozens of railroad companies were based in Chicago. In 1850, the Illinois and Michigan Canal connected Chicago to the Mississippi River. Trade that had once headed to St. Louis, Missouri, came to Chicago instead.

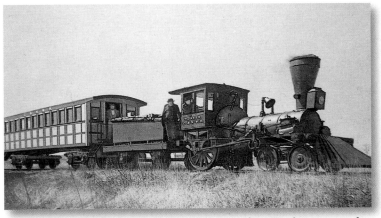

Chicago's first locomotive was the Galena and Chicago Union Railroad's "The Pioneer"

William Le Baron Jenney designed the Home Insurance Building. It was made from steel instead of concrete, allowing for more windows.

The country's first high-rise was built in Chicago. Made with a steel frame instead of traditional stone, the 10-story Home Insurance Building was constructed in 1885. It was light and fire-resistant. This new style gave birth to the architectural movement called Chicago School. It used steel frames, elevators, and electric lights. Architects of this period would have been amazed to learn that one day Chicago would have the second tallest skyline in the United States (New York City having the tallest). By 2023, Chicago had five of the fifteen tallest buildings in the country.

A New Century

By 1900, more than 1.7 million people were living in Chicago. It was one of the fastest growing cities in the world. These early years of the 20th century would see another influx of citizens. Mexican immigrants began to move to Chicago in significant numbers during this time, often settling the Pilsen and Little Village neighborhoods. The Great Migration, in which millions of African Americans moved from the South to Northern cities to escape more harsh racial segregation and seek new jobs., began in 1916. It lasted for much of the 20th century, and transformed Chicago's South and West Sides into vibrant cultural hubs with significant musical, artistic, and civil rights contributions.

Despite this growth, the city had long dealt with waterborne diseases like typhoid. Water polluted by sewage and waste mixed with Chicago's drinking water. City officials decided that the polluted water had to flow west toward the Des Plaines River, instead of east toward Lake Michigan. It was one of the most challenging problems ever faced, but once again Chicago accomplished an amazing feat of engineering. It took eight years, 8,500 workers, and a lot of newly invented

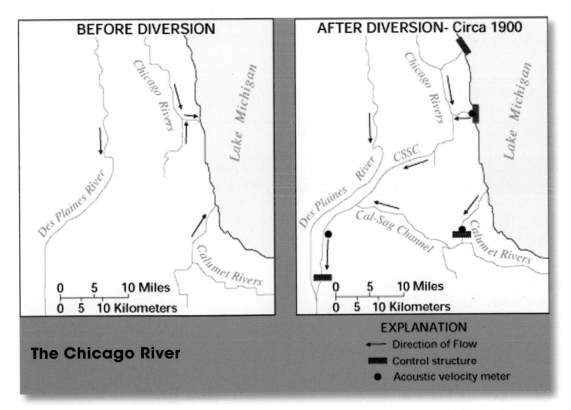

The Chicago River

Changing the direction of an entire river is a massive task, but the city managed to do it.

The new canal was literally a lifeline for Chicago that allowed the city to grow without endangering the health of the citizens.

Construction of the impressive Chicago Sanitary and Ship Canal involved using new earthmoving inventions along with more traditional techniques.

earthmoving equipment to do it, but Chicago successfully reversed the flow of the Chicago River.

The project, known as the Chicago Drainage Canal and later as the Chicago Sanitary and Ship Canal, was the largest public works project ever at the time. They dug up over 4 million truck loads of dirt and rock and created a canal that's bigger than the Panama Canal and wider than the Suez Canal.

Today, the Chicago River features multiple bridges, allowing drivers to easily cross to either side. On St. Patrick's Day, this river is dyed bright green in honor of the city's many Irish immigrants.

The beauty of the landscape and buildings of Chicago's World's Fair inspired people from across the world. Could cities really look like this? Daniel Burnham, the Director of Works for the fair and a Chicago architect specializing in city planning, was sure Chicago could be that beautiful. In 1906, he was asked to work out a new city plan. What he came up with over the next three years changed the face of Chicago.

Daniel Burnham (top) believed everyone should live within walking distance of a park.

PLAN OF
CHICAGO
PREPARED UNDER THE DIRECTION OF
THE COMMERCIAL CLUB
DURING THE YEARS MCMVI, MCMVII, AND MCMVIII

BY
DANIEL H. BURNHAM
AND
EDWARD H. BENNETT
ARCHITECTS

EDITED BY
CHARLES MOORE

CHICAGO
THE COMMERCIAL CLUB
MCMIX

The Burnham Plan and Beyond

How can you design a modern, exciting city? By studying other cities, of course! That is what Daniel Burnham did to put together a plan for Chicago. He and his business partner Edward Bennett studied some of the greatest cities to see how they were arranged.

Burnham took his time. He worked on his plan for three years. Finally, in 1909, he presented the Burnham Plan to city officials. He had designed it to be much like the European cities he had seen. The new design included plans for:

- improving the city's beautiful lakefront area,
- developing a complex and efficient highway system,
- improving the train systems,
- rearranging city streets,
- creating a row of city parks connected by tree-lined pathways, and
- establishing a civic center for government officials.

A look at Chicago today shows how many of Burnham's ideas are still in place, from the band of parks along the city's waterfront to the steady flow of traffic on some of the city's busiest highways. With more than 600 parks in Chicago, Burnham reached his goal of having every Chicagoan within walking distance of a park.

Some of the changes involved shifting the names of streets and changing house numbers. That was no small chore. Eventually all even-numbered addresses were located on the north or west side of a street. Odd-numbered ones were on the south or east side. Streets

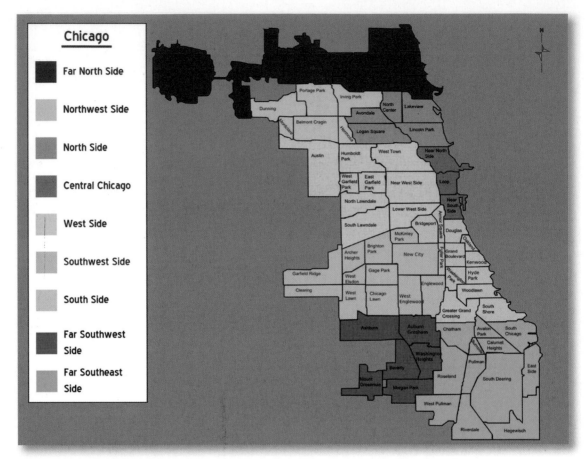

Chicago neighborhoods at the time streets were changed.

running north and south were all called avenues. Those running east and west remained streets. While the changes made sense, they also caused confusion—especially for mail carriers.

In 1914, poet Carl Sandburg wrote the poem "Chicago." It begins:

Hog Butcher for the World,
Tool Maker, Stacker of Wheat,
Player with Railroads and the Nation's Freight Handler;
Stormy, husky, brawling,
City of the Big Shoulders

Wrigley Field, home of the Chicago Cubs, was built in 1914. It is known for its ivy-covered brick outfield wall and the unpredictable wind off Lake Michigan.

These words describe how the city had grown and developed, gaining strength from its industries. It continued to expand. It added more parks and movie theaters. It built museums and aquariums. It constructed sports stadiums and airports.

The Windy City began to be known for a rich sports culture and passionate fan base. It's had an array of famous sports teams over the years, including cross-town rivals the Chicago Cubs and the Chicago White Sox. The Cubs were once famous for a 108-year championship drought. Their win in the 2016 World Series broke the streak. Chicago is also home to the successful Chicago Bulls of the NBA, the often-Stanley Cup-winning Blackhawks, and the NFL's Chicago Bears. The Bears were one of the founding member teams of the NFL.

Shedd Aquarium was built between 1927 and 1929 and opened in 1930. Twenty railroad tank cars took eight round trips between Key West and Chicago to haul one million gallons of seawater for the saltwater exhibits.

As Chicago's footprint and skyline changed, the population constantly grew and shifted, as well. By 1920, more than two million people lived there. During the 1840s, many Irish Catholics came to the area, forced from their homeland by the Great Famine. By the end of the century, the railroads, stockyards, and other labor industries employed skilled workers from throughout Europe, including Germany, England, Sweden, and Norway. Former slaves moved from the segregated South to find jobs in the North.

As more migrants moved to Chicago, tensions grew between the ethnic groups. In 1919, a weeklong race riot killed 38 people and injured over 500. Ten years later, Irish-American and Italian-American

Originally from New York, Al Capone became synonymous with Chicago crime.

gangsters clashed in lethal battles over bootleg whiskey and illegal gambling territory. Seven Irishmen were killed in the St. Valentine's Day Massacre of 1929, and Italian gangster Al Capone rose to power. Riots and protests over civil rights issues continued through the next few decades.

Taking the "L"

In the late 1890s, Chicago's streets were busy. Horses, carriages, carts, streetcars, and people created traffic jams. Something had to be done to speed things up and clear the streets. In 1892, the city built the "L." This steam-powered train went 3.6 miles in 14 minutes on raised tracks.

People watch marathon runners pass under the "L." These train tracks stretch for hundreds of miles. They make commuting easier and lessen traffic problems in key places in the city.

("L" stands for "el," short for "elevated.") On the train's first run, many people scrambled to close their curtains as passengers looked into their second- and third-story windows.

This first steam-powered "L" train helped transport the thousands of workers and visitors to the World's Fair. It was replaced by an electric-powered train. Soon the city built more train lines. By 1897, four trains circled the city in a large loop (known as "The Loop"). Over the last century, the system was modernized. Wooden cars were replaced with metal ones. Air-conditioning was installed. Human conductors lost their jobs to machines.

Today, the "L" is considered one of the seven wonders of Chicago. Its eight lines cover more than 224 miles. On average, over 300,000 people ride it every weekday.

Frank Lloyd Wright

Frank Lloyd Wright

Oak Park, a suburb of Chicago, was for many years the home of one of the world's greatest architects of the 20th century: Frank Lloyd Wright. Today, years after he designed and built them, his buildings are considered classics. His "Prairie School" style echoed the flatness of the Midwestern landscape, and houses made in that style are found throughout Oak Park. Wright put an emphasis on the horizontal, with strong detail added in the wooden siding and high bands on the windows. Roofs were low, and terraces and balconies were prominent features. Wright loved nature and often designed his homes so that occupants could easily access the outside.

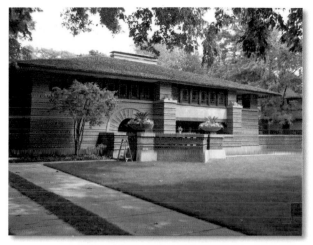

The Heurtley House

Perhaps his most famous work in Chicago is the Rookery Building lobby. It is considered the oldest standing high-rise in Chicago. Wright redesigned the lobby in 1905, adding wrought iron and marble finishes. The building is one of the primary places architecture fans visit in Chicago.

The Rookery Building

More than 25,000 people visit the Willis Tower every single day. From the observation deck, on a clear day, tourists can see Indiana, Illinois, Michigan, and Wisconsin.

Chicago, Today and Tomorrow

Every year, about 49 million people come to Chicago to visit. Traveling around the city can be an adventure. Besides the "L" train, there is the Pedway, a pedestrian walkway system. This series of tunnels and bridges links 40 blocks of downtown. It is a great way to get from place to place while staying dry and warm. You can also take a taxi. There are more than 7,000 of them within the city limits. In addition, Uber and Lyft services are available.

Soaring high above the city is what used to be known as the Sears Tower. Today it is called the Willis Tower. Built in 1973, it was the world's tallest building at the time. (At 110 stories, it had the most floors in the world until the 160-story Burj Khalifa was finished in 2010.) In order to have enough space to construct it, Sears had to buy 15 surrounding buildings—and an entire street. Construction took three years and 2,000 workers. It used the same amount of concrete as an eight-lane, five-mile-long highway. The tower weighs 445 million pounds. That is the same as 20,000 city buses! It has more than 16,000 windows that are regularly cleaned by six robotic roof-mounted window-washing machines.

Each year, 1.7 million tourists stop by the tower's Skydeck. From there, they can see all of Chicago—and also into the neighboring states of Wisconsin, Michigan, and Indiana. Two daredevils have scaled the Willis Tower. Both made it—and both were arrested when they reached the top.

Another city attraction is Navy Pier. Although Burnham had hoped to build five piers on the lake, Navy Pier was the only one completed. It opened in 1916. Over the years, it has served as a prison for World War I draft dodgers, a World War II training center for Navy pilots, and a home for the University of Illinois. Today the pier offers its almost 9 million annual visitors restaurants, shops, sightseeing cruises, and a one-acre indoor botanical garden. Here you can enjoy the sight of 80 live palm trees under six stories of glass and arched ceilings.

No visit is complete without a ride on the pier's famous Ferris wheel. It has 42 gondola cars. Each one holds eight to ten passengers. Less than one year after it opened in 2016, the almost 200-foot-tall Ferris wheel had carried more than 1 million people into the Chicago sky.

One of the city's most popular spots is Millennium Park. It opened in 2004 and covers almost 25 acres. The site used to be a railroad yard and parking lot. Now it has a huge outdoor music auditorium with a high-tech sound system. There are several fountains, including

The colorful Navy Pier has food and activities both inside and out.

the Crown Fountain. It has two towers that have water cascading down them. Images of faces are projected on the towers. When the eyes and mouths open, a long gush of water pours out, delighting children and other visitors.

Also in Millennium Park is *Cloud Gate*—better known as "The Bean." The creator, Indian-British architect Anish Kapoor, wanted to make something that looked like a drop of liquid mercury. It would reflect both the sky and the city skyline. "What I wanted to do . . . is make something that would engage the Chicago skyline," Kapoor says in the audio tour, "so that one sees the clouds kind of floating in, with those very tall buildings reflected in the work."

The Jay Pritzker Pavilion in Millenium Park is a beautiful, high-tech gathering place.

Although Kapoor named his sculpture Cloud Gate, people immediately began calling it the Bean because it is shaped like a kidney bean. The sculpture has an internal frame with flexible connectors and an outer skin formed of stainless steel panels. While the original sculpture contained a small construction office, later the Bean was welded shut to make it appear seamless. The sculpture was unveiled on May 15, 2006. It is 66 feet long and 33 feet tall. To keep it so incredibly shiny, it is wiped down and power washed every single day. The sides are so shiny and the reflections so clear that it is easy to walk right into the sculpture and "get beaned by the Bean."

Chicago's Bean can trick the eyes. It can be hard to figure out which way to walk when near it. It has been featured in a number of movies, including *Source Code*.

The Adler Planetarium, founded in 1930, is part of Chicago's impressive Museum Campus. As of 1987, it is a National Historic Landmark.

Chicago continues to attract newcomers from all over the globe. It has huge museums and planetariums for exploring the wonders of the world. It features sports stadiums for watching favorite teams play. It has hundreds of parks for picnics and zoos for watching exotic wildlife. In a city with a history as rich and long as Chicago's, it is easy to see why, even without a World's Fair going on, people want to visit it—and sometimes, stay for good.

Chronology

Early History   The Kickapoo, Miami, Ottawa, Potawatomi, Shawnee, Winnebago, and other Native American groups live in the area that is now Chicago.

1673   Father Jacques Marquette and Louis Jolliet arrive from France.

1803   Fort Dearborn is built. It is destroyed in 1812 and rebuilt in 1816.

1837   The town of Chicago is incorporated as a city.

1845   The Great Famine prompts hundreds of thousands of people to leave Ireland over the next four years. Thousands of them move to Chicago.

1848   Chicago's first railroad is built.

1850   The Illinois and Michigan Canal is built to connect Chicago to the Mississippi River.

1854   Cholera kills thousands of people in Chicago.

1855   Chicago hires engineer E.S. Chesbrough of Boston to solve the city's sewage problem. To install the sewers, the city begins raising all the buildings 4 to 14 feet.

1858   The Chicago Fire Department is established.

1871   The Great Chicago Fire destroys thousands of buildings and kills more than 300 people. Building codes are rewritten to prevent further fires of this size.

1874   Another fire destroys 800 buildings. Stricter building codes are put into place to use less wood in construction.

1885   The Home Insurance Building becomes the world's first high-rise.

1893   The Columbian Exposition, or Chicago World's Fair, is held from May through October.

1897   The Loop Elevated Line ("L") is completed.

1900   To protect drinking water from sewage, engineers reverse the flow of the Chicago River.

1909   The Burnham Plan for the city is completed.

1914   Carl Sandburg publishes the poem "Chicago."

1915   On July 24, the *SS Eastland* capsizes at the dock in Chicago; 844 people perish.

1916   Navy Pier opens.

1919   A race riot breaks out between ethnic groups.

1929   After the St. Valentine's Day Massacre, Al Capone becomes the most powerful gangster in Chicago.

1955   Chicago's O'Hare Airport officially opensto commercial passenger service. Richard J. Daley is elected mayor. During his 21 years in office, he oversees programs that strengthen the city's neighborhoods.

1973   The Sears Tower is built.

Chronology

1989 Richard M. Daley, the son of Richard J. Daley, is elected mayor. During his 22 years in office, he will improve the city's public schools and public housing, construct Millennium Park, and expand O'Hare International Airport.

1997 Chicago announces that the Great Chicago Fire was not the fault of the O'Learys or their cows.

2004 Millennium Park opens.

2005 The Chicago White Sox win their first World Series in 88 years.

2006 Cloud Gate, better known as "The Bean," opens in Millennium Park.

2009 The Sears Tower is renamed the Willis Tower.

2015 Chicago Blackhawks win the Stanley Cup for the third time in six years.

2016 Navy Pier's Centennial Wheel (the new Ferris wheel) opens. The Cubs win the World Series for the first time in over a century.

2018 Architects continue to build soaring skyscrapers throughout the city, including the 70 story, 836 foot tall One Bennett Park. It offers 69 condos and 279 apartments.

2019 Lori Lightfoot becomes the city's first female African-American mayor.

Books

Art Institute of Chicago. *Treasures of the Art Institute of Chicago: Paintings from the 19th Century* to the Present. New York: Abbeville Press, 2018.

Lewis, Anna. *City Doodles Chicago.* Layton, Utah: Gibbs Smith, 2013.

Sutton, Patricia. *Capsized! The Forgotten Story of the SS Eastland Disaster.* Chicago: Chicago Review Press, 2018.

Tarshis, Lauren. *I Survived the Great Chicago Fire*, 1871. New York: Scholastic, 2015.

Works Consulted

City of Chicago: "Chicago History." https://www.chicago.gov/city/en/about/history.html

City of Chicago: "Cultural Affairs and Special Events: Millennium Park—Audio Tours: Cloud Gate."https://www.chicago.gov/content/dam/city/depts/dca/mpaudio/ CloudGate.mp3

Grossman, Ron. "The First Chicago Elevated—or 'El'—Opens." *Chicago Tribune*, December 19, 2007. https://www.chicagotribune.com/news/nationworld/ politics/chi-chicagodays-firstelevated-story-story.html

Janega, James. "Reversing the Chicago River (1900)." *Chicago Tribune*, October 29, 2013. https://www.chicagotribune.com/business/blue-sky/chi-reversing-chicago-river-1900-innovations-bsi-series-story.html

Further Reading

Keppler, Nick. "9 Reflective Facts about Chicago's Cloud Gate." *Mental Floss*. May 14, 2016. https://mentalfloss.com/article/79961/9-reflective-facts-about-chicagos-cloud-gate

LaTrace, AJ. "The Exclusive One Bennett Park Tower Rises above Chicago." *Chicago Magazine*, April 19, 2018. https://www.chicagomag.com/real-estate/april-2018/the-exclusive-one-bennett-park-tower-rises-above-chicago/

Marshall, Colin. "The World's First Skyscraper: A History of Cities in 50 Buildings, Day 9." *The Guardian*, April 2, 2015. https://www.theguardian.com/cities/2015/apr/02/worlds-first-skyscraper-chicago-home-insurance-building-history

Sandburg, Carl. "Chicago." *Poetry*. March 1914. https://www.poetryfoundation.org/poetrymagazine/poems/12840/chicago

Schons, Mary. "The Chicago Fire of 1871 and the 'Great Rebuilding.'" *National Geographic*, January 25, 2011. https://education.nationalgeographic.org/resource/chicago-fire-1871-and-great-rebuilding/

Sheehan, Charles. "MP3 Tour Download: A Walk in the Park." *Chicago Tribune*, July 1, 2005. https://www.chicagotribune.com/chi-0507010212jul01-story.html

Stranahan, Susan Q. "The Eastland Disaster Killed More Passengers Than the Titanic and the Lusitania. Why Has It Been Forgotten?" *Smithsonian Magazine*. October 27, 2014. https://www.smithsonianmag.com/history/eastland-disaster-killed-more-passengers-titanic-and-lusitania-why-has-it-been-forgotten-180953146/

Sulski, Jim. "Who's on First? Jolliet, Marquette." *Chicago Tribune*. October 26, 1997. https://www.chicagotribune.com/news/ct-xpm-1997-10-26-9710260140-story.html

Young, David. "Raising the Chicago Streets Out of the Mud." *Chicago Tribune*, December 18, 2007. https://www.chicagotribune.com/nation-world/chi-chicagodays-raisingstreets-story-story.html

Zukowsky, John, et al. "The Plan of Chicago: 1909–1979." The Art Institute of Chicago. 1980. http://m.artic.edu/sites/default/files/libraries/pubs/1980/AIC1980PlanofChicago_comb.pdf

On the Internet

American Historama: "Chicago World's Fair" https://www.american-historama.org/1881-1913-maturation-era/chicago-world-fair.htm

Ducksters: "The Great Chicago Fire" https://www.ducksters.com/history/us_1800s/great_chicago_fire.php

Kids Konnect: "Chicago Facts & Worksheets" https://kidskonnect.com/places/chicago/

Social Studies for Kids: "The Great Chicago Fire of 1871" https://www.socialstudiesforkids.com/articles/ushistory/greatchicagofire18711.htm

Glossary

bootleg whiskey—Alcohol made and/or sold during Prohibition (proh-hih-BIH-shun), when it was illegal.

cholera (KAH-lur-ah)—A deadly disease caused by a germ that lives in dirty drinking water. It infects the small intestine.

draft dodger—Someone who avoids getting drafted into the army at wartime.

Great Famine (FAM-in)—The hunger caused in Ireland between 1845 and 1849 when potato crops failed. Around one million people starved to death, and hundreds of thousands of people left Ireland to start new lives in other countries.

metropolis (meh-TRAH-puh-lis)—A large city.

missionary (MIH-sheh-nayr-ee)—A person who travels to do church work.

sculpture (SKULP-chur)—A piece of artwork carved or molded, usually from wood, rock, or metal.

segregated (SEH-greh-gay-ted)—Separated according to race.

sewage (SOO-idj)—Waste matter from sinks and toilets.

typhoid (TY-foyd)—A sometimes fatal illness caused by a germ in old food or dirty drinking water. It causes headaches, nosebleeds, and a fever that can last up to three weeks.

Index